SURF SMART: STAYING SAFE ONLINE

Cody Crane

Children's Press®
An imprint of Scholastic Inc.

Thank you to our expert content consultant:
Heidi Julien, Ph.D.
Professor and UB Exceptional Scholar – Sustained Achievement
Department of Information Science
University at Buffalo SUNY

and our educational consultant:
Jackie Fego
Science Liaison
C.V. Starr Intermediate School
Brewster, NY

Library of Congress Cataloging-in-Publication Data available

ISBN 978-1-5461-7818-7 (library binding) | ISBN 978-1-5461-7819-4 (paperback) |
ISBN 978-1-5461-7820-0 (ebook)

10 9 8 7 6 5 4 3 2 1 26 27 28 29 30

Printed in China 62
First edition, 2026

Design by Kathleen Petelinsek
Series produced by Spooky Cheetah Press

Find the Truth!

Everything you are about to read is true ***except*** for one of the sentences on this page.

Which one is **TRUE**?

TRUE or FALSE Cyberbullying is the same as real-life bullying.

TRUE or FALSE A strong password should contain letters, numbers, and symbols.

What's in This Book?

Introduction 6

1 Smart Choices

How can you steer clear of harmful people and information online? 9

2 Protect Your Privacy

What can you do to keep your private information safe? 15

The BIG Truth

Are You Ready for a Phone?

Take this quiz to find out if you could handle the challenges.......................... 24

A phone is a big responsibility.

What do you know about website cookies?

3 Do Not Be Fooled

How can you avoid being tricked by online scams? 27

4 Beware of Bullies

What should you do if you meet an online bully? 35

Email Detective 40

What Would You Do? 42

True Statistics 44

Resources 45

Glossary 46

Index 47

About the Author 48

Look for this symbol throughout the book. Pause and reflect to answer the questions.

Passwords:
~~12345678~~
~~qwerty~~
~~abcdefg~~
✓GingerBreadRocks99$$

It is important to learn how to make a strong password.

INTRODUCTION

The internet is an amazing tool. It links computers, phones, and other digital devices around the world. People of all ages use it to learn new things and connect with one another. Where else can you **do research for homework**, **chat with friends**, **watch videos**, **play games**, and **shop**? But the internet also comes with risks. In this book, you will learn how to stay safe online by avoiding dangerous people and information, keeping your **private** details **safe**, avoiding online scams, and handling online bullying. Get ready to **Surf Smart**!

Playing online games with real-life friends is safe.

How much time do you spend online per day? Do you think it is too much?

The number one thing most kids do online is watch videos.

There are a lot of things online to grab your attention.

CHAPTER

1

Smart Choices

Billions of people use the internet. That means you could run into many strangers online. There are also more than a billion websites to visit and millions of apps to download. As a result, you might come across lots of new things—some of which are not meant for kids. Making good decisions online can help you avoid dangerous people and harmful content.

Set Some Ground Rules

The best way to figure out what websites and apps are safe for kids is with help from trusted adults. They can also help you learn which websites and apps to stay away from. So grab your grown-up and go over these basic internet rules.

1. Always ask an adult before using a device to go online. If possible, use the device together.
2. Let your adult know what you plan to do online and only visit websites and use apps they say are OK.
3. Do not download anything without your adult's permission.
4. Only email, message, and chat with people you know in real life.

Why do you think you should use only websites and apps a trusted adult has approved?

More than 70 percent of all kids have come across something inappropriate online.

Right for You?

You are watching a video online when an ad for a scary movie starts to play. Yikes! You quickly close the app playing the video. You did the right thing. Leave a site or turn off your device if anything makes you feel uncomfortable. Some content online is inappropriate for kids. It might be frightening or violent, or contain hateful or bad language. If you see something online that upsets you, talk to your adult. They can help you make sense of it.

Who Is It?

A player messages you privately during an online game. They say they are a kid your age and they want to be friends. But they might not be who they say they are. If they ask you to do anything that makes you feel uncomfortable, like giving them personal information or pictures of yourself, tell a trusted adult right away. And never agree to meet someone you met online in person.

Why might it be safer to play games online only with people you know in real life?

Do not respond to messages from strangers online.

Your Best Behavior

You visit a website, share an image, and comment on a friend's post. All this online activity is now part of your **digital footprint**. This trail of online information can shape how others view you. You cannot permanently delete something bad or embarrassing you share on the internet. So always think about whether your actions online present the best version of yourself.

How do you want people to see you online?

Keeping certain information private can help you stay safe.

CHAPTER

2

Protect Your Privacy

The internet is a useful tool for sharing ideas, hobbies, and likes and dislikes. These types of personal information can be fun to talk about with others. You may find out that you have many things in common with lots of other people. But not all personal information is safe to share online. Anything that could be used to identify you personally should be kept private.

What personal information do you think should not be shared online?

Should You Share It?

You should not share anything online that you would not tell a stranger in real life. Below are some examples of personal information that is OK to share and private information that is not.

OK to Share	Not OK to Share
Photos that you have taken of pretty scenery or animals	Identifying information, like your full name or birth date
Favorite things, like books, foods, songs, and movies	Contact information, like your email address or phone number
Things you have in common with others, like your shoe size or number of siblings	Your location, like your home address or the name of your school
Successes, like winning a soccer game or earning a scouting badge	Financial information, like a credit card number
Projects, like something you have built or art you have created	Passwords, usernames, and answers to **security questions**

Password
IloveCats123

What is something about yourself that would be OK to share online?

Keep in mind that some sites are just for adults.

You must be 13 years old or older to use most **social media** sites. Why do you think that is?

Sign Me Up?

There is a cool new app you want to use. But it says you need an adult's permission to create an **account**. Apps and websites made for kids under 13 years old require an adult's **consent** before you can use them. That is because you will need to provide some private information, like your email address. You must sign up for these accounts with an adult. It is the only time you can give out private information online.

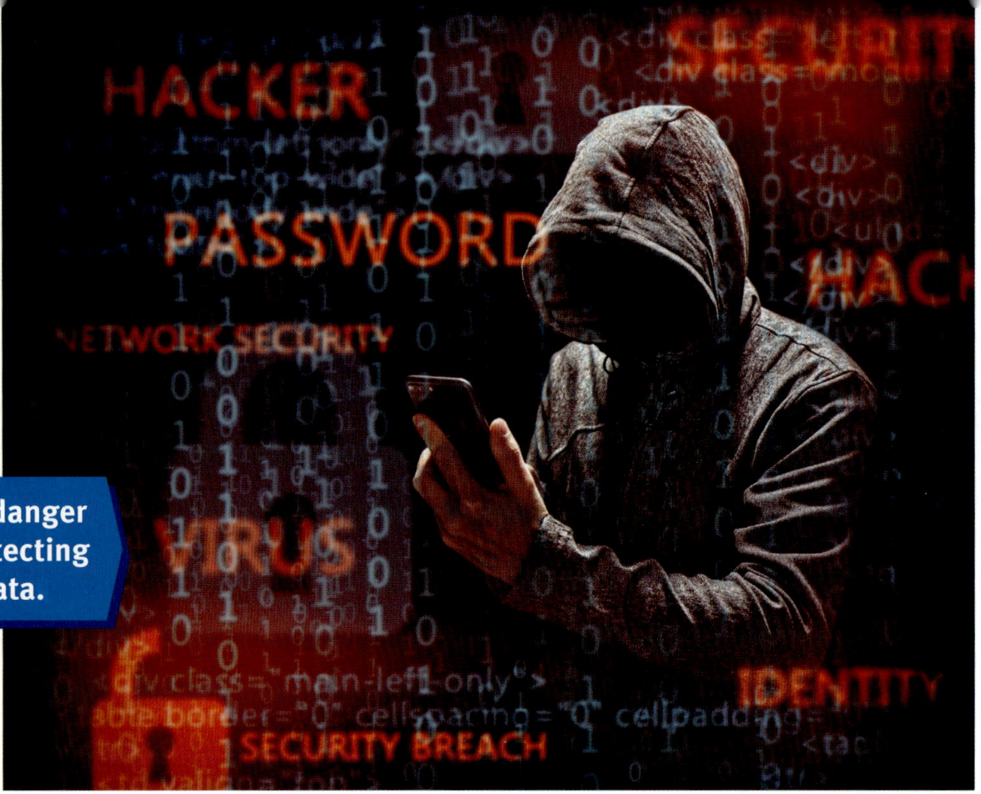

Avoid danger by protecting your data.

The Danger

If someone finds out your private information, they could use this **data** in harmful ways. They could unlock a device used by your entire family if they learn its password. Then they could find out more private information. Or they could discover your home address and try to steal things in real life.

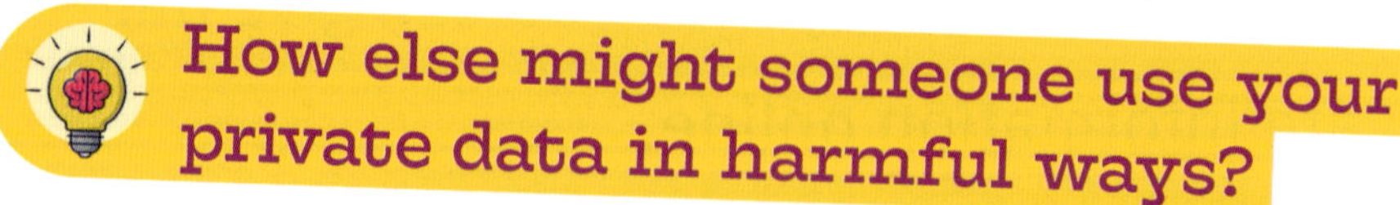

Stolen Identity

One big reason to keep your private information safe is to prevent **identity theft**. That is when a **hacker** uses your private data to pretend to be you online. They might do all sorts of illegal things. For example, they might open a credit card account in your name and rack up a huge bill. You could end up getting in trouble for something someone else did with your private data.

Almost 10 percent of Americans have their identity stolen every year.

Identity theft is when someone pretends to be you.

Security Check

You need to make sure the apps, web browsers, websites, and devices you use are secure. They all have privacy settings that control what personal information these tools can access or share with others. An adult can change these settings to block access to your personal photos and location. Or they can limit who sees things you post online so only friends and family can see them—instead of anyone on the internet.

It is important to check the privacy settings on all your devices.

Why might you not want a device to share your location with everyone?

Build a Better Password

Nearly every digital device and online account requires you to create a password. Passwords safeguard your private information, so it is important to make them strong. Use the tips on this page to create a password that would be tough for someone to guess.

Password Tips

1. Do not use personal information like the name of a pet or your favorite sports team as a password. Someone could easily figure it out based on everyday facts you post online.
2. Do not make your password too simple. It should be at least 12 characters long and include a mix of upper- and lowercase letters, numbers, and symbols.
3. A password needs to be something you can remember. That might be a favorite saying or phrase that relates to you.

Passwords:

~~12345678~~

~~qwerty~~

~~abcdefg~~

✓ GingerBreadRocks99$$

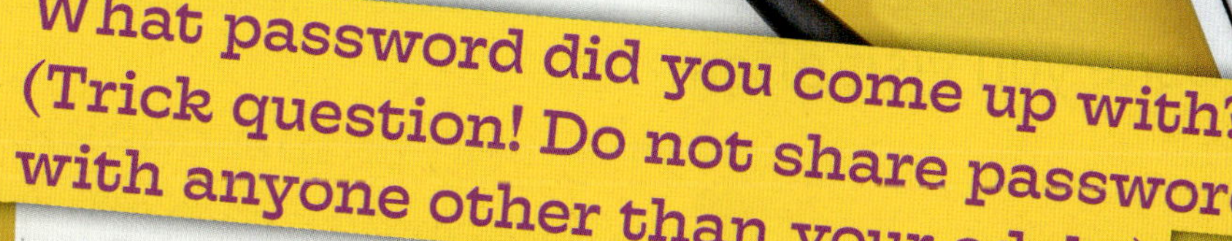

Cookies track your online activities.

Not-So-Tasty Cookies

In real life, cookies are sweet baked treats. But online, cookies are bits of information saved by websites. Cookies allow the site to remember data about you. That includes if you have visited in the past, items you are shopping for, passwords, and even credit card numbers. You will often see a message when you visit a website. It will ask if you would like to allow cookies. Say no, unless it is a trusted website you visit often.

Do you think cookies are helpful in any way?

Spying on You?

Websites also use cookies to collect data about you without you knowing. The cookies are used to track what you click on while on the site. Web browsers use similar tools to monitor what you search for and sites you visit. This allows them to show you ads with products you might be interested in. Advertising is the way many websites make money.

About 40 percent of all websites use cookies.

Websites can make money by collecting information about you.

The BIG Truth

Are You Ready for a Phone?

Smartphones are the devices kids use most to go online. And many kids cannot wait until they can get their own. But having a phone is a big responsibility. So, many experts say it is best to wait until you are in high school to get one. Use the questions on the right to see if you might be ready for your own phone.

START

Are you good at taking care of your things? Phones are expensive. It could be a big deal if you lose your phone or break it.

NO

YES

Are you good at following rules at home and at school? Your adult will likely have rules about when and how you can use a phone.

NO

YES

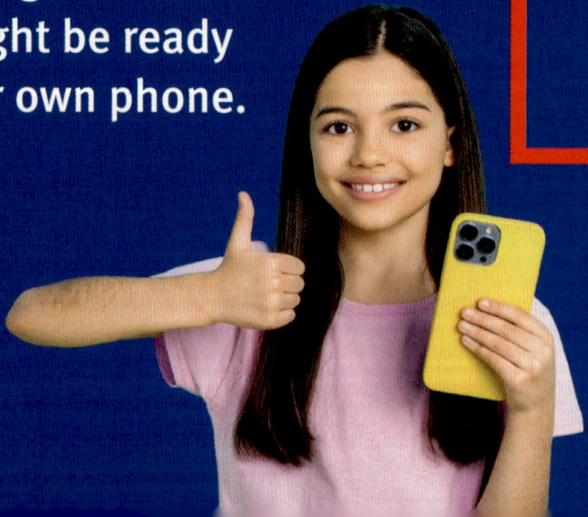

Do you understand the importance of staying safe online? You know not to give out private information or talk to strangers.

NO → You are not ready for a phone.

YES ↓

Can you limit your screen time and balance it with other activities? Phones can be distracting. You need to be able to turn the phone off and do more important activities.

NO → You are not ready for a phone.

YES ↓

Do you know how to avoid inappropriate content and handle cyberbullying? You visit only sites that are meant for kids and where users are respectful to others online.

NO → You are not ready for a phone.

YES ↓

Are you responsible with your homework and chores? You get all your work done before using your phone for fun.

NO → You are not ready for a phone.

YES ↓

You might be ready for a phone. Talk to your adult to see what they think.

You are not ready for a phone.

If you already have a phone, do you think you should keep it?

Remember: You cannot win a contest you did not enter.

CHAPTER

3

Do Not Be Fooled

You are on a website and suddenly a burst of confetti appears on the screen. A colorful banner says, “Congratulations! You have WON a PRIZE!” Do not get too excited. This is likely a **scam**. Hackers do not just wait for you to share private data by accident. They use tricks, like lying about a free prize, to fool you into giving them this information. The good news is there are ways to make sure you do not fall for these traps.

Why should you be suspicious of something online that seems too good to be true?

Spam Alert

You check your email and see a new message. But you do not recognize who sent it. The email is likely spam. Sometimes businesses send these unwanted emails as ads. But hackers also send spam emails that can contain harmful **computer programs**. Clicking on a link in the email might accidentally download the programs to your digital devices. That can allow hackers to get into your device and steal private information.

The word *email* is short for electronic mail.

Don't even open an email from someone you don't know.

The first computer virus was created in 1971.

The fastest-spreading computer virus in history shut down 500,000 computers in a single week in 2004.

Is My Computer Sick?

One harmful computer program used by hackers is called a virus. It infects a device and can destroy its data or cause it to stop working. Other programs allow hackers to take control of your device. They can even allow a hacker to watch you through your camera! Check that the green light next to your device's camera is off when not in use. That means no one is using it to spy on you. Or to be extra safe, when you're not using your device's camera, put a sticker over it.

Fishing for Info

DING! You get an email or a text that claims to be from a popular online store. The message says the company needs some information to complete your order. You click on a link and it takes you to a page that looks like the store's website. But it is a clever fake! This scam is called phishing (FISH-ing). If you enter your personal data into the website, it will be stolen.

How do you think phishing scams got their name?

Timeline: A History of the Internet

1971
The first email is sent between computers.

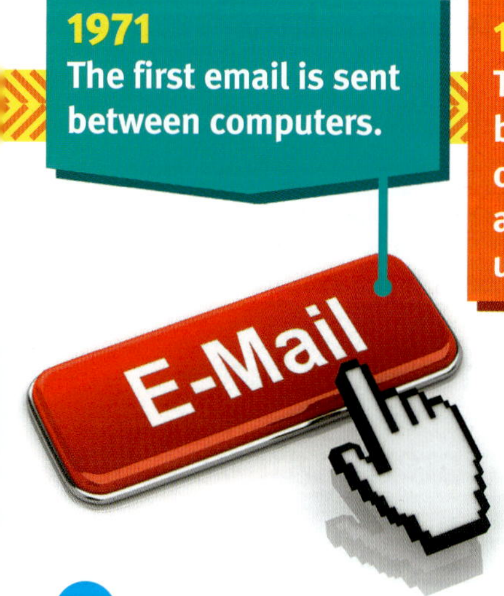

1983
The internet is born, connecting computers at several universities.

1991
The first website is created. It explains what the internet is!

1993
The first web browser to search the internet is introduced.

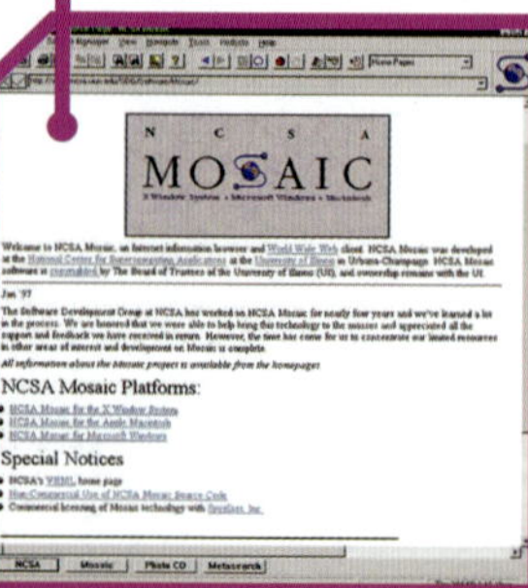

Pop-Up Warning

People dislike pop-up ads so much, their inventor once apologized for creating them!

While visiting a website, a small window pops up on your screen. It says, "WARNING! Something is wrong with your computer. Click here." This box is a pop-up. Many websites use them to show ads or get people to sign up for their sites. But hackers use pop-ups too. And when you click, the pop-up downloads a dangerous program to your device. Or it takes you to a site that tries to trick you into giving personal information.

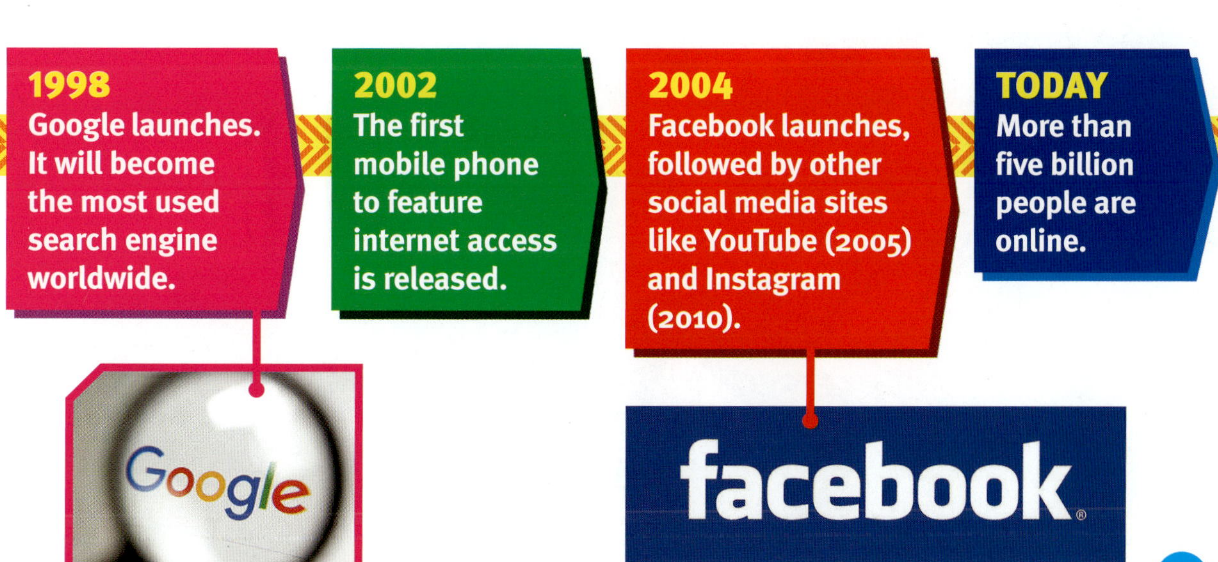

Safety Net

If you surf the internet on a computer, ask an adult to install a computer program to block unwanted ads. That will keep pop-up scams from appearing. They can also install a program to detect viruses and other harmful tools used by hackers. They can block websites that might be security risks too.

Your adult can help make sure you do not fall victim to a scam.

Spotting a Scam

It can be very hard to spot a scam. But being aware helps a lot. Always check these things before opening any email, text, or link.

Online scams are usually run by large groups of people as an illegal business.

It might be a scam if . . .

1. You do not recognize a person's name, number, or email address.
2. The subject of an email is all capital letters, or has lots of exclamation marks, or the email has words misspelled.
3. An email claims to be from a business, but the email address does not contain the company's name.
4. A URL—the address of a website—seems unusual. For example, it has an odd spelling of a familiar website's name.

It does not matter where bullying happens; it is never OK.

CHAPTER

Beware of Bullies

You are chatting online about your favorite TV show. Then a classmate makes fun of you for watching it. Ugh! They are being so mean! Using the internet to post hurtful things or send mean texts is an example of cyberbullying. Being bullied online or in real life can have a negative effect on your **mental health**. It can make you feel stressed, sad, lonely, and bad about yourself.

How would you feel if someone said or did something mean to you online?

Meanness Online

It can be easier for people to be mean online than in person. That is because they cannot see how their behavior is making others feel. They also might be less worried about getting in trouble. Here are the steps you should take when faced with a bully online.

1 Tell an adult.

2 Do not reply right away.

3 When you're ready, tell the bully, either online or in person, that you don't like how they are behaving and that they should stop.

About 15 percent of kids in the United States ages 9 to 12 say they have been bullied online.

Real Life vs. Online

Cyberbullying happens when someone uses technology to harass, upset, or embarrass another person. Because it happens online, it can occur more often to more people than bullying in real life. Here are some other ways real-life bullying and cyberbullying differ.

Real-Life Bullying	Cyberbullying
It usually happens face-to-face, often in secret.	It includes messages sent directly to a person, as well as those posted online that many people can see.
It can include physical threats, like pushing, hitting, or damaging someone's personal property.	Posting personal information or something embarrassing about someone, teasing and name-calling, and spreading rumors are all examples of bullying that can happen online.
It is usually limited to a specific location, like school.	Because the bullying is online, you can feel it wherever you are.
The bully is someone you know.	A bully online can be anyone, and they may keep their identity hidden.
Usually, one person or a small group does the bullying.	Everyone who can see the bullying online can join in.

Before you say anything online, ask: Would I say this to the person's face?

Zero tolerance means bullying is never allowed.

Most cyberbullying occurs on social media apps and through text messages.

Not Allowed

Many apps and websites have rules against online bullying. They offer ways to report or block a bully. Schools often have zero tolerance for any kind of bullying—online or off. If you are a victim of online bullying, you should report it to a teacher or your trusted adult right away. And save the bully's messages. This is important proof to share.

Safe Place for All!

Great job! You have learned about the dangers online and what to do to avoid them. You know how to keep your private data secure and identify scams. And you know how to handle bullies and when to ask an adult for help. By playing it safe online, you will help make the internet a better place for everyone!

Do you feel more confident about using the internet now that you know how to stay safe online?

The internet can help bring people closer together.

Email Detective

To start this activity, cover page 41 with a sheet of paper or a large book. Done? Now, please continue reading! Something about this email looks fishy. There are five clues that tell you it is a scam. See if you can find them all. If you need help, go to page 33. Then check the answers on page 41.

Subject: PROBLEM WITH YOUR YOUTUBE ACCOUNT!!!!!!!
Mon, 1:00AM

From: Smith, Zack <zack12299@email.com>

Hi,
We need you to update your account. Please use this link: www.utub.com or open the attachmint below for more information.
Thank you,
Zack

1 Attachment
File: open.exe

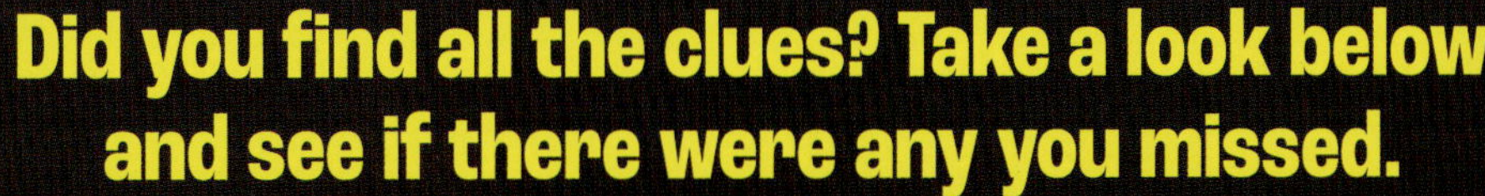

The subject line is in all capital letters with lots of exclamation points to get your attention.

The email address does not have the company's name.

Subject: PROBLEM WITH YOUR YOUTUBE ACCOUNT!!!!!!!
Mon, 1:00AM

From: Smith, Zack <zack12299@email.com>

The email is asking you to update private information.

Hi,
We need you to update your account. Please use this link:
www.utub.com or open the attachmint below for more information.
Thank you,
Zack

1 Attachment
File: open.exe

Words are spelled wrong.

The website does not match the company's name.

What Would You Do?

Just like in real life, the things we say and do online can affect how a person feels. Read the examples below of behaviors that would be considered cyberbullying. How would you react in each situation? See if it matches the "What to Do" solution given.

POSTING SOMETHING EMBARRASSING: At a sleepover, a kid takes a video of someone snoring. They share it online because they think it is funny.

WHAT TO DO: Explain that posting an embarrassing video of someone online would hurt their feelings. Tell them to delete it.

TEASING AND NAME CALLING: While chatting with friends online about meeting up to play soccer, one person calls another a "slowpoke." They say they do not want them on their team.

WHAT TO DO: If someone is making fun of someone else, do not join in. Tell others to stop as well. Invite the person to be on your team.

HURTFUL GAMING: A friend says you should steal all the loot a classmate collected in an online game.

WHAT TO DO: Say no. If someone did something mean to your online character, you would be upset. Instead, keep the game fun for everyone.

And don't forget: Tell a trusted adult any time you see cyberbullying!

SPREADING RUMORS: Someone sent you an email with a mean rumor about a classmate.

WHAT TO DO: Do not forward the message to other kids in the class. And tell the original sender that they should not post lies or gossip online.

True Statistics*

- **Percentage of the world's 8 billion people that use the internet:** 69%
- **Average amount of time kids in the United States, ages 8 to 10, spend online per day:** 6 hours
- **Percentage of content online made specifically for kids:** 20%
- **The amount online scams cost people around the world in 2023:** $8 trillion USD
- **Percentage of emails people receive that are spam:** 46%
- **Two of the most common passwords in the world:** "123456" and "password"
- **The number of visits the busiest website, Google, sees in a month:** 83 billion

As of 2024

Did you find the truth?

FALSE Cyberbullying is the same as real-life bullying.

TRUE A strong password should contain letters, numbers, and symbols.

Resources

Other books in this series:

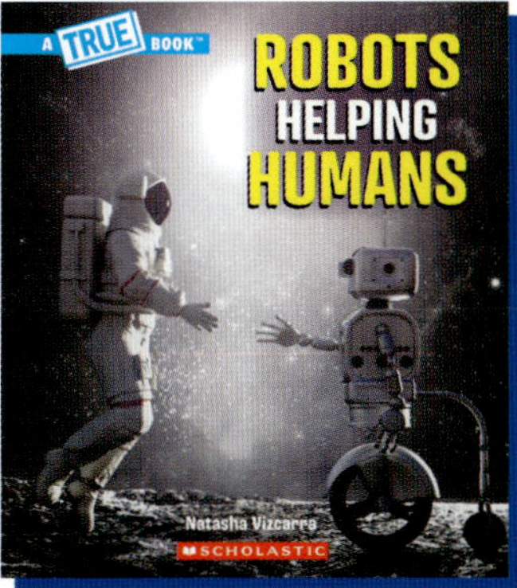

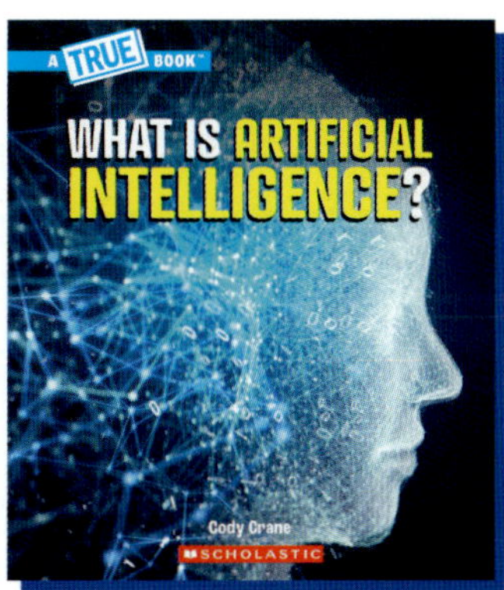

You can also look at:

Cook, Julia (author) and Anita DuFalla (illustrator). *The Technology Tail: A Digital Footprint Story*. Boys Town, NE: Boys Town Press, 2017.

Pearlman, Catherine. *First Phone: A Child's Guide to Digital Responsibility, Safety, and Etiquette*. New York: TarcherPerigee, 2022.

Speer, Jessica (author) and Lesley Imgart (illustrator). *The Phone Book: Stay Safe, Be Smart, and Make the World Better with the Powerful Device in Your Hand*. Sanger, CA: Familius, 2023.

Thaler, Nina Du. *Diary of Elle: Cyber-Safety Can Be Fun*. Brisbane, Australia: Bright Zebra, 2015–2019.

Glossary

account (uh-KOUNT) a personal profile created to use a website, an app, or another online service

computer programs (kuhm-PYOO-tur PROH-gramz) series of instructions, written in a computer language, that control the way a computer works

consent (kuhn-SENT) official agreement

data (DAY-tuh) information collected in a place

digital footprint (DIJ-i-tuhl FUT-print) the trail of data a person leaves online

hacker (HAK-ur) someone who has a special skill for getting into a computer system without permission

identity theft (eye-DEN-ti-tee THEFT) the crime of wrongfully obtaining or using another person's personal data through fraud or deception, often for financial gain

mental health (MEN-tuhl HELTH) the condition of your mind and emotions

scam (SKAM) an act meant to deceive someone

security questions (si-KYOOR-i-tee KWES-chuhnz) questions that are used to confirm a user's identity

social media (SOH-shuhl MEE-dee-uh) websites and applications that let users create online communities in which they participate in social networking or share messages, videos, and other content

Index

adult assistance, 10, 11, 12, 17, 20, 32, 36, 38, 39, 43
age restrictions, 17

cameras, computer, 29
computer programs, harmful, 28–29, 32
cyberbullying, 34–38, 42–43

digital content, 11
digital footprint, 13

email, 10, 28, 30, 33, 40–41, 43

hackers, 19, 27–29, 31, 32

identity theft, 19
inappropriate content, 11

mental health, 35

online presence, 13
online safety, basics of, 6, 9–13, 39

passwords, strength of, 18, 21
personal information, sharing of, 15–17
phishing, 30
phones, decisions about, 24–25
pop-up advertisements, 31–32
privacy protection
  importance of, 14–15, 18–19
  security practices for, 20–23, 26–33
  when sharing personal information, 15–17

reputation, protecting, 13

safety on internet, basics of, 6, 9–13, 39
scams, 6, 26–33, 40–41,
security settings and programs, 16, 20, 32
sharing personal information, 15–17
social media, 17, 38, 42
spam, 28, 30, 33, 40–41
strangers, 6, 9, 10, 12, 16
surveillance, online, 22–23, 29

text messages, harmful, 30, 33, 35, 38
theft of personal information, 18, 19, 27–33

viruses, computer, 29, 32

website cookies, 22–23

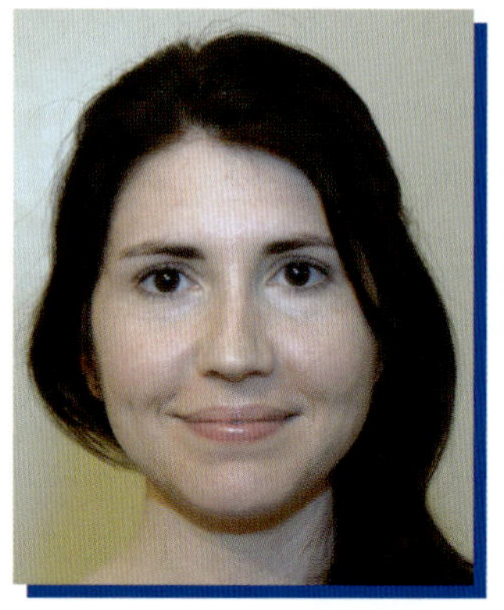

About the Author

Cody Crane is an award-winning nonfiction children's writer. Her favorite subjects to write about are science and art. She plans to read this book with her ten-year-old son to help keep him safe online!

Photos ©: cover: metamorworks/Getty Images; back cover: Portra Images/Getty Images; 5 bottom: Wirestock/Getty Images; 6–7: Smederevac/Getty Images; 8–9: SDI Productions/Getty Images; 10: Yurii Sliusar/Getty Images; 11: Iuliia Burmistrova/Getty Images; 12: Narumon Bowonkitwanchai/Getty Images; 13: stop123/Getty Images; 16 left: Ariel Skelley/Getty Images; 16 center left: SDI Productions/Getty Images; 16 center right: Calvin Chan Wai Meng/Getty Images; 16 right: goir/Getty Images; 17: ilkercelik/Getty Images; 19: Portra Images/Getty Images; 21: Wirestock/Getty Images; 23: Marco_Piunti/Getty Images; 26 foreground: John Kevin/Getty Images; 29: scanrail/Getty Images; 30 center: CERN; 30 right: National Center for Supercomputing Applications/University of Illinois Board of Trustees/NSF; 31: Moritz Wolf/imageBROKER.com/Alamy Images; 34–35: Jatuporn Tansirimas/Getty Images; 36 left: Daisy-Daisy/Getty Images; 36 top right: Peter Berglund/Getty Images; 36 bottom right: StockPlanets/Getty Images; 37: Halfpoint Images/Getty Images; 38: Lindsey Nicholson/UCG/Universal Images Group/Getty Images; 39: Ariel Skelley/Getty Images; 40–41: alexsl/Getty Images; 42 left: Imgorthand/Getty Images; 42 right: Lane Oatey/Blue Jean Images/Getty Images; 43 left: Addictive Stock/Getty Images; 43 right: shapecharge/Getty Images; 44: Wirestock/Getty Images.

All other photos © Shutterstock.